kijc

W9-DEC-027

THE STORY BEHIND
DAY OF THE DEAD

MELISSA RAÉ SHOFNER

PowerKiDS press

New York

Published in 2020 by The Rosen Publishing Group, Inc.
29 East 21st Street, New York, NY 10010

First Edition

Editor: Tanya Dellaccio
Book Design: Reann Nye

Photo Credits: Cover, p.1 Windzepher/iStock Editorial/Getty Images Plus/Getty Images; pp. 4, 6, 8, 10, 12, 14, 16, 18, 20, 22 (background) Preto Perola/Shutterstock.com; pp. 5, 11 Dina Julayeva/Shutterstock.com; p. 7 Cintia Erdens Paiva/Shutterstock.com; p. 9 Tomasz Guzowski/Shutterstock.com; p. 13 Kobby Dagan/Shutterstock.com; p. 15 Gabriel Perez/Moment/Getty Images; p. 17 John Block/Blend Images/Getty Images; p. 18 Angela Ostafichuk/Shutterstock.com; p. 19 Fer Gregory/Shutterstock.com; p. 21 jvmodel.com/Shutterstock.com; p. 22 CassandraMoHer/Shutterstock.com.

Library of Congress Cataloging-in-Publication Data

Names: Shofner, Melissa Rae, author.
Title: The story behind day of the dead / Melissa Rae Shofner.
Description: New York : PowerKids Press, 2020. | Series: Holiday histories |
 Includes index.
Identifiers: LCCN 2018054386| ISBN 9781725300408 (pbk.) | ISBN 9781725300422
 (library bound) | ISBN 9781725300415 (6 pack)
Subjects: LCSH: All Souls' Day–Juvenile literature. | Mexico–Social life
 and customs–Juvenile literature.
Classification: LCC GT4995.A4 S56 2020 | DDC 394.266–dc23
LC record available at https://lccn.loc.gov/2018054386

Manufactured in the United States of America

CPSIA Compliance Information: Batch #CSPK19. For Further Information contact Rosen Publishing, New York, New York at 1-800-237-9932.

CONTENTS

A Happy Holiday

Day of the Dead sounds scary—but don't be afraid! This holiday is a happy time during which people honor their loved ones who have passed away. Families gather to **celebrate** with tasty foods, big parties, and even fun parades.

Honoring the Dead

Long ago, many early peoples in South America and what we now call Mexico believed it was **disrespectful** to be sad about people who had died. Many groups honored their **ancestors** by celebrating them in different ways. The ancient Aztecs, for example, held parties and **festivals** during the month of August.

Many years later, in the 1500s, the Spanish took over Mexican land. They made many Mexican peoples switch to Catholicism, which was the **religion** practiced by the Spanish. Catholics celebrate All Saints' Day on November 1 and All Souls' Day on November 2 to honor their dead loved ones.

Two Days of Celebration

Day of the Dead—or Día de los Muertos, as it's called in Spanish—became a mix of the Catholic holidays and the **traditional** Mexican celebrations. To make sure the dead aren't disrespected, their families honor them over two days each year: November 1 and 2.

On November 1, people celebrate the lives of children who have died. They leave white flowers on the children's **graves**. Adults who have died are honored on November 2. On this day, people leave orange flowers called marigolds on graves.

Leaving Offerings

In places that celebrate Día de los Muertos, people believe that their dead loved ones come back to the land of the living to celebrate with their families. People set up tables called *ofrendas* with candles, flowers, and offerings for the dead.

15

Food and Drinks

To help the dead on their trip to the world of the living, people prepare and leave out traditional Mexican food and drinks. Sometimes these offerings are what the ancestor loved to eat and drink most when they were alive.

Pan de muerto, or bread of the dead, is a type of sweet bread made for Day of the Dead. People also make pure sugar candies in the shape of **skulls** to honor the dead. Sugar skulls were first made in Mexico around the 1700s.

Life of the Party

Day of the Dead celebrations may also include a big party in the **cemetery**. People often **decorate** their loved ones' graves. One decoration you might see at a Day of the Dead celebration is *papel picado*, which is colorful paper with pictures cut into it.

Celebrating Today

Day of the Dead is a fun and happy celebration meant to honor dead ancestors, but it's also about reminding people that death is part of life. It's celebrated mostly in Mexico, but people in other countries celebrate, too.

GLOSSARY

ancestor: Someone in your family who lived long before you.

celebrate: To do something special or enjoyable for an important event or holiday.

cemetery: A place where dead people are buried.

decorate: To make something look nice by adding something to it.

disrespectful: Showing that you don't think someone or something is valuable or important.

festival: A gathering for a special occasion.

grave: A hole in the ground for burying a dead body.

religion: The belief in a god or a group of gods.

skull: The bones that form the head and face of a person or animal.

traditional: Following what's been done for a long time.

INDEX

WEBSITES

Due to the changing nature of Internet links, PowerKids Press has developed an online list of websites related to the subject of this book. This site is updated regularly. Please use this link to access the list: www.powerkidslinks.com/HH/dead